Brilliant
BRAI

Brilliant
BRADFORD

Telegraph & Argus

breedon **books**
PUBLISHING

First published in Great Britain in 2008 by
The Breedon Books Publishing Company Limited
Breedon House, 3 The Parker Centre,
Derby, DE21 4SZ.

ISBN: 978-1-85983-623-1

Printed and bound by Progress Press, Malta.

Contents

Foreword

BRADFORD is one of the most under-rated cities in Britain – perhaps not least by many of its own citizens. A one-time industrial powerhouse, one of the engines of the Industrial Revolution, its wool industry created fabulous wealth for the Victorian mill owners and merchants who used the proceeds to build magnificent municipal edifices, commercial buildings and grand homes.

We lead such busy lives today that we rarely take time to pause and study our surroundings, which is why so many residents and workers fail to appreciate the glory, splendour and richness of our built heritage. Bradford has a stunning and varied array of buildings, many carved from mellow Yorkshire stone. In all, the district has more than 5,800 Listed buildings, including around 20 Grade I and more than 60 Grade II* structures.

This tremendous display is not the end of the story, though: Bradford is forging ahead with a multi-billion pound regeneration which is already contributing some fine modern architecture to the skyline.
Our photographers – GREGG BROWN, ANDREW GARBUTT, ANTHONY McMILLAN, LUCY RAY and MIKE SIMMONDS – have striven to throw new light on the scene for residents and visitors alike. I am indebted to them and their colleagues SIMON WAITES, DAVID BARNETT and STEVE SPENCER for all their hard work and creativity in bringing this book together.

We could not hope to capture all the wonderful buildings in Bradford in one book, but we hope we have provided a representative sample – enough, we believe, to give an interesting and inspiring insight into the glory that is *Brilliant Bradford.*

Perry Austin-Clarke
EDITOR
Telegraph & Argus

Most of the images featured are available to buy on our website:
www.telegraphandargus.co.uk

CITIES are in a constant state of flux. They have to be, because the city that stands still eventually lies down and dies. Not all of the planning decisions that have redrawn the landscape of Bradford city centre have been universally welcomed – witness the widespread regret at the demolition of the beautiful Swan Arcade in the 1960s – but Bradford, at the end of the first decade of the 21st century, does finally appear to be reaching a happy medium between preserving the past and looking to the future. Architect Will Alsop, deemed by some to be a 'maverick', gave the modern Bradford a springboard to consider bold, new designs with his master plan for the city centre. Things are progressing, with schemes such as the proposed city park incorporating a mirror pool, the canal project to reopen a waterway into the city centre and the Broadway shopping centre all in various stages of development. But the regeneration is in sympathy with that which has gone before, and Bradford's proud heritage can be seen in every block of Yorkshire stone as it catches the unique light of a sun rising on one of the country's most constantly evolving and mighty cities.

A new city is being born right in the heart of Bradford. To the tens of thousands of Bradford inhabitants who pass by it every day, the Broadway site is termed 'the hole in the ground'. But, at the time of writing, preparatory work by developer Westfield had begun on this huge swathe of land in the centre of Bradford *(right)*. From it will rise a new shopping centre, with Debenhams, Marks and Spencer and several high-street names signed up already.

Below right: A bird's-eye view of Centenary Square, which lies at the foot of City Hall, one of the oldest buildings in Bradford. Centenary Square was officially opened by the Queen on 27 March 1997, and the area regularly hosts fairgrounds, markets and special events, including performances of classical concerts and opera beamed directly to the big screen, erected there to show live matches from the World Cup in 2006.

Below: A view taken from the frontage of the Impressions Gallery and Bradford 1 Gallery.

The newly-built home for bars, restaurants and the art galleries, nicknamed 'the concrete banana' for its yellowish façade and curving shape, dominates one side of Centenary Square. It contains the Impressions Gallery, a mainly photographic gallery, which relocated to Bradford from York. It also houses the Bradford 1 Gallery, which shows off some of the treasures owned by the city's museums' department.

Right: The weather vane is a reminder of Bradford's industrial past. An alpaca, famed for its wool, sits on top of the weather vane, which is positioned on the roof of Conditioning House on Canal Road, where wool in its raw state was unloaded.

Left, clockwise from top left: From Bank Street, looking towards the shops which will back on to the huge Broadway development; Hall Ings, one of the busy thoroughfares around the city, with traffic heading towards the Jacob's Well pub and the roundabout that shares its name; crocuses pushing up through the grass, looking towards Nelson Street; a domed tower on Britannia House at the end of Broadway.

Below: The clock tower of City Hall dominates the background, while at the front old and new mix together. The building at the centre is a former bank, now – with a firm acknowledgement of the past – the Old Bank pub. To the right are the windows of apartments, evidence of the growth of city-centre living in Bradford.

Nestling behind the trees is the Tyrls – the former police station.

Bank Street and the Broadway site by night.

The Argus Chambers on Hall Ings.

The *Telegraph & Argus* glass-encased press hall.

Forster Square was built in the late 19th century and was a public garden and transport interchange until 1958; now it gives its name to this nearby retail park.

The arch at the bottom of Ivegate was built in 1988 to represent Bradford life.

The former Yorkshire Penny Bank.

Ivegate, a narrow, steep street of shops and pubs.

One of the many mosques that dot the city's skyline. This one is on North Parade.

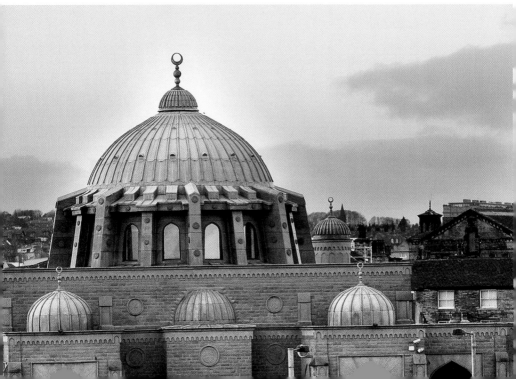

Bradford or Budapest? An atmospheric shot of Hustlergate.

A view of the Great Victoria Hotel and St George's Hall, across the roof of Bradford Interchange.

The subway, leading to the Interchange from Bridge Street.

A shot of the glass roof. This has been a transport hub since 1850, becoming the Interchange in 1983 after a bus station was added to existing rail services in 1977.

This page sees the building and cloisters of the former Belle Vue Boys' Grammar School on Manningham Lane, now a private girls' school called Coral College. It was built in 1895 and was also used as Manningham Middle School. The Grade II listed building can count Bradford writer J.B. Priestley as one of its alumni.

Opposite, clockwise from top left: The *Telegraph & Argus* building, which occupies land between Hall Ings and Drake Street; a domed tower on the former Rawson Hotel; the Leisure Exchange, a recent addition to the city-centre landscape, on Vicar Lane; sunshine falling through greenery outside the Tyrls.

One can spend a long time looking up at the Church Institute building on North Parade, with its excellent collection of heraldic carvings, gargoyles and gothic-style canopies. Formerly the base of the Church Literary Institute, it held a lecture room and a library. The Grade II listed building was constructed in the 1870s and has latterly still been used for religious purposes and also as a coffee shop.

The old Yorkshire Penny Bank has endured as one of Bradford's most loved landmarks since it was built in 1895. Now a Grade I listed building, it has even inspired the sincerest form of flattery – across the junction, the Sovereign Health Care building is a mirror image of its domed roof. As a bank, it pioneered savings accounts for school children and offered one of the first chequebook services. During times of unemployment, it also functioned as a soup kitchen, and in recent years it has housed restaurant and pub businesses. There are more pictures of the building on the following pages.

27

Sunbridge Road is one of Bradford's main thoroughfares and the subject of much development in recent years, with new apartments being built and shops opening. At the top of the page is the view from the bottom of Sunbridge Road to Tyrrel Street, where some examples of the architecture (pictured above) can be spied along the road.

An aerial shot of the start of Sunbridge Road from Centenary Square.

A whole generation of Bradfordians felt a little bit of their childhood disappear when it was announced that the Co-op was pulling out of Sunwin House, at the top of Sunbridge Road. The department store had been a mainstay of the city since its opening in 1935, but in November 2004 owners United Co-operatives decided to sell up. The building is now occupied by retailer T.J. Hughes.

Below: Detail on one of the many fine buildings that line Sunbridge Road. This one is Waller's Buildings, which occupies No.44 and was built in 1879.

There are some unexpected architectural surprises around any corner in the city centre. *Top left:* Some fine Art Nouveau railings fronting the Trades Hall on Sunbridge Road. These were the premises of one of the first modern trades unions in the country – the Amalgamated Dyers' Society, which was formed in 1878 from what was the Amalgamated Operative Dyers' Accident, Burial and Trade Protection Society.

Top Right: A stained-glass window on Sunbridge Road.

Left: La Plata House on Sunbridge Road, so-called because it was the offices of a company that had dealings with South America – La Plata is in Argentina.

Right: This elegant building is the Bradford Register Office on Manor Row, where marriages have been conducted, deaths registered and births recorded for more than 135 years. The foundation stone was laid in 1876 after the building was commissioned by the Board of Guardians of the Bradford Poor Law Union as their headquarters.

Below: This impressive structure at the bottom of Leeds Road, near Eastbrook Hall in Little Germany, has recently been revitalised as sought-after apartments in a development known as the Reading Rooms.

Traditional Bradford in the shape of the Station Hotel pub on Manchester Road meets up-to-the-minute technology as one of the blocks of flats towers over it. The Manchester Road blocks have been fitted with wind turbines to generate sustainable energy.

Bradford University, seen in all its glory in the aerial photograph *(top)*, has recently been the subject of some innovative development, including the distinctive atrium *(above and left)*. Made with the same high-transparency foil that graces the Eden Project in Cornwall, it was described as a 'jewel inserted into an urban fabric' by judges of an architectural awards scheme in 2007.

Little Germany

TAKE just a short walk from the city centre and it can feel as though you have stepped through a portal to another world. Little Germany's streets are sometimes quiet canyons carved from the Yorkshire stone buildings that rear up on either side. In reality, those streets were carved from commerce and entrepreneurship. Founded in the 19th century as the warehousing district for the exporting of the fruits of Bradford's wool trade, many of the businesses that settled in Little Germany were European and, more specifically, German. Fronted by the imposing Eastbrook Hall, this little district is a draw for tourists who like to wander along its shaded streets and find themselves delighted by an unexpected piece of street sculpture. It is also something of an arts hub, with the Priestley Theatre situated there. Redevelopment of many of the old buildings into top-class apartment blocks, plus the addition of bold new builds such as the Gatehaus, only add to Little Germany's slightly bohemian feel. And with the impending Broadway development set to refocus the retail heart of Bradford City Centre, Little Germany will find itself increasingly centre stage.

Top left: The aerial picture shows the extent of the compact area known as Little Germany. In the bottom of this picture, fronting onto the road, is Eastbrook Hall, undergoing redevelopment as apartments. Further along to the right is the distinctive shape of the recent Gatehaus development.

Left: Looking back to the city centre.

The pictures on this page show the scale and imposing nature of many of the buildings that make up Little Germany, while on the following pages there are close-ups of some of the intricate and often intriguing details carved into the doorways and window ledges around the area.

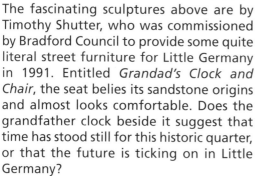

The fascinating sculptures above are by Timothy Shutter, who was commissioned by Bradford Council to provide some quite literal street furniture for Little Germany in 1991. Entitled *Grandad's Clock and Chair,* the seat belies its sandstone origins and almost looks comfortable. Does the grandfather clock beside it suggest that time has stood still for this historic quarter, or that the future is ticking on in Little Germany?

Right and Opposite: More examples of the intricate carvings on the building façades.

Little Germany is the place where the old and new truly collide.

Left: A dizzying worm's-eye view of the Gatehaus building from the courtyard at the centre of the 35m tall, 11-storey development that cuts a swathe through the clean lines and square blocks of Little Germany's rigid grid system, like an Art Deco ocean liner. Comprising more than 130 apartments and penthouses, the Gatehaus is a fine example of the recent and welcome trend of people moving back to living in Bradford city centre.

Opposite and below: Some fine examples of Little Germany's more traditional architecture.

The impressive Gatehaus building.

Cathedral

BRADFORD Cathedral, which overlooks the city from its partially hidden vantage point near Little Germany, has a long and illustrious history stretching back as far as the seventh century. Saxon crosses found on the site indicate that Christians may have worshipped there, dating back to the mission of Paulinus to Northumbria in AD627. Raiders from Scotland are thought to have burnt a chapel to the ground that stood there in the 14th century, and the building that replaced it survived, in some form, the Dissolution of the mid-16th century. It played its part in the English Civil War when the royalist Earl of Newcastle famously laid siege to the city, and there were various programmes of rebuilding and refurbishment in the 19th and 20th centuries. Today, it is a lively and active part of Bradford's daily life.

This page shows a view of the tower and an example of the many wonderful stained-glass windows in Bradford cathedral. Among them are finely detailed works showing the birth, death and rebirth of Christ.

Right is another view of the tower which was completed in 1508 and stands 100ft tall. It survived bombardment by the royalists in 1642, and it housed the very first public clock in Bradford.

The Nave – this part of the cathedral dates back to the 15th century, and the roof uses timbers from Tong Forest. The angels just peeking from the shadows may have links to Kirkstall Abbey, near Leeds.

Some more examples of architectural and design details from the cathedral.

Bradford Cathedral holds some fine examples of the stained-glass work of William Morris (1834–1896), an artist and writer who was one of the founders of the British Arts and Crafts movement. He and his daughter May were also among Britain's very first socialists. He is perhaps better known for his wallpaper designs, many of which are reproduced to this day. The Lady Chapel at Bradford Cathedral boasts one of the earliest commissions of Morris's work in its East Window. The work was carried out in 1863 and reset a century later.

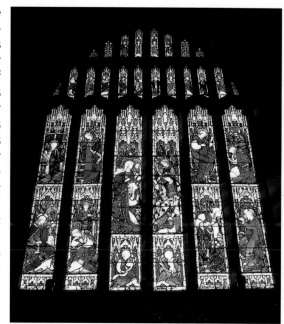

I am he that liveth and was dead and behold I am alive for evermore. Amen

Richard Fawcett who died May 8th 1845

Despite its size and regular use for services and special events, Bradford Cathedral seems to demand at least a moment of quiet contemplation from anyone who passes through its ancient portals.

Details of some of the fine sculpture work that counterpoints and complements the cathedral's grand scale.

City Hall

IT WAS Queen Victoria who united the towns of Bradford, Manningham, Horton and Bowling as a single borough, back in 1847. These entirely separate communities needed a headquarters for their single governing body, and for the first 26 years of this new community's life the freshly minted council met in Swain Street in Bradford. It soon became apparent that meeting in a fire station was not sufficient for this rapidly growing borough, and the site on which City Hall now stands was acquired in 1869. The design of the new building was thrown open to all, much in the way that new developments in regenerating Bradford are put out to tender. The winners, local architects Lockwood and Mason, came up with the design that was created by builders John Ives and Son of Shipley at a cost of £100,000 – for which you would struggle to get even the smallest one-bedroomed apartment in the city centre today. Three years later, the building was open for business.

Bradford in bloom...City Hall seen through the fragrant spring blossoms in white and pink *(above and below)*, and with a carpet of glorious red tulips at the Jacob's Well roundabout *(opposite)*.

Left and above: The famous clock tower.

City Hall, framed by the Hall Ings footbridge ramp.

The Town Hall, as it was until November 1965, rapidly outgrew its boundaries following its building, and by the end of the 19th century it was decided to expand it. By 1909 it had a new council chamber and committee rooms, and in 1914 a redesigned entrance was added. Throughout the years, these impressive gargoyles looked on as Bradford grew and grew around it. Yet another facelift followed in 1965 when the Town Hall became a City Hall. Also at roof level are two flagpoles, which are used to mark commemorative events such as national or saints' days, to respect deaths of civic dignitaries and to mark Royal visits.

Perhaps the most famous 'inhabitants' of City Hall – well, certainly of its exterior – are the statues that watch over the city, high up above the cloistered entrances *(above)*.

This page shows James II *(right)* and William III *(far right)*.

Opposite, top row, from left to right: Charles II, Edward VI, Queen Mary. *Bottom row, from left to right:* Henry V, Henry IV, Henry VII.

Above: Oliver Cromwell (unlike the others, not a monarch)

Left, top row, from left to right: William IV, George IV, George III.
Bottom row, from left to right: Henry I, William II, Queen Anne.

As well as sound, City Hall is associated with light.

The Ferris wheel on one of the many Centenary Square fairgrounds.

The light of the clock shines across Bradford.

City Hall is imaginatively lit for the closing of the Illuminate arts festival in 2006.

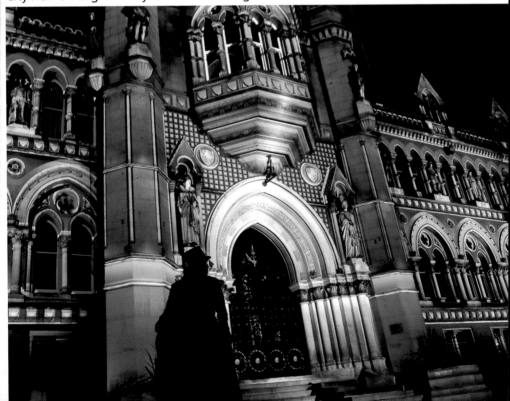

The City Hall clock tower rises 220ft above ground level. It was inspired by the Palazzo Vecchio in Florence, Italy, and has 13 bells, which fell silent for five years in 1992 due to decay, but a National Lottery grant helped get them ringing again.

Left: City Hall from the corner of Centenary Square and Bridge Street.

Right: The view from Nelson Street.

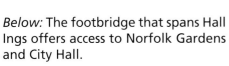

Below: The footbridge that spans Hall Ings offers access to Norfolk Gardens and City Hall.

The true scale of the clock tower can be seen in this imposing shot from Market Street.

Courts

THE site where Bradford's Law Courts now stand, between the Great Victoria Hotel and Hall Ings, was once the scene of very different activity. In 1850 a station was opened there by the Lancashire and Yorkshire Railway. Three decades later it was completely rebuilt and served the city for almost a century, until it was relocated just across the road in what is now the Bradford Interchange. The Law Courts were built in 1990 and deal with all kinds of judicial proceedings, including criminal cases, civil processes, family courts, youth hearings and divorces. Over at the far end of Centenary Square is the Magistrates' Court. This building was opened by Her Majesty The Queen in 1974, along with the Tyrls. In 2007 a plan was set in motion to relocate the Magistrates' Court to a new site, alongside the Law Courts on Exchange Square, creating a judicial hub off Drake Street. The demolition of the quintessentially 1970s building on Centenary Square would make way for ambitious plans to create a city park incorporating a mirror pool, as per architect Will Alsop's vision for regenerating Bradford.

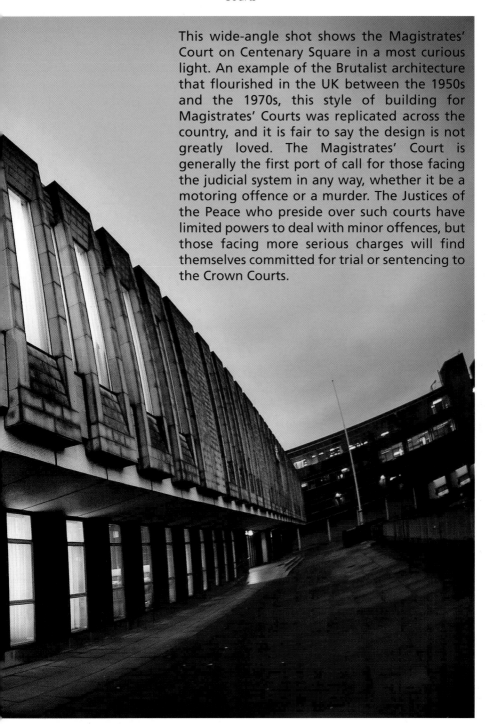

This wide-angle shot shows the Magistrates' Court on Centenary Square in a most curious light. An example of the Brutalist architecture that flourished in the UK between the 1950s and the 1970s, this style of building for Magistrates' Courts was replicated across the country, and it is fair to say the design is not greatly loved. The Magistrates' Court is generally the first port of call for those facing the judicial system in any way, whether it be a motoring offence or a murder. The Justices of the Peace who preside over such courts have limited powers to deal with minor offences, but those facing more serious charges will find themselves committed for trial or sentencing to the Crown Courts.

Established in 1990, the Law Courts moved from their former premises on Manor Row, a building currently being redeveloped into city-centre apartments. Clad in stone, designed to complement the rest of the city centre's architecture, the square that is laid out in front of the building is lined with trees *(right)*. Contrast the design with that of the Magistrates' Court *(below)*, a structure of concrete and glass.

Opposite: An unusually quiet Law Courts, perhaps at the end of the day's proceedings or maybe before the numerous lawyers, barristers, judges, ushers, clerks, police officers, witnesses and defendants arrive.

The colonnade effect of the columns and lamps on the Law Courts on Drake Street.

The entrance to the Law Courts.

FROM the modern comforts of worldwide chains, such as the Hilton and the Holiday Inn, to the charms and traditions of grand old establishments, such as the Midland and the Great Victoria, Bradford, like any major city, is well catered for with hotels. The city's history – especially its popular culture – was cemented in part in the hotels of the city, while Bradford's contention to be a major 21st-century hub for business and leisure is evidenced through the number of global brands that make their home here...with more to come, as the Broadway retail and leisure development is currently ongoing. The playwright George Bernard Shaw once said that 'The great advantage of a hotel is that it is a refuge from home life'. While none of us want to spend too long away from home, there is certainly enough in Bradford's historic hotels to pique our interest for as long as we have to.

The Great Victoria Hotel, looking out on to Bridge Street and the Interchange in one direction and the Law Courts in the other, is one of the grandest buildings in Bradford. It was built in 1867, during the reign of the Queen whom it honours with its name, and has been one of Bradford's most enduring businesses and landmarks ever since. In the early days it was where wealthy merchants stayed when in the city to conduct their business; over the years its clientele has morphed to take in modern-day captains of industry, political leaders (Conservative leader David Cameron held a Shadow Cabinet meeting there in February 2008), and pop stars and actors appearing at the nearby St George's Hall or Alhambra Theatre.

The Victorians knew the secret of combining the massive scale of building with intricate, almost delicate, detailing. These are the elaborate sculptings around the cornices and pillars on the fascia of the Great Victoria, with the lion looking proudly down near the Drake Street sign above the entrance to the Corniche Bar, situated within the hotel.

The entrance to the Corniche Bar and Grill.

A close-up of the enduring Victorian architecture of this much-loved building.

Across the city, on the edge of Forster Square, is the grand Midland Hotel, completed in 1890 by the Midland Railway Company as their showpiece hotel. You would have to go to London to see architecture like this, especially the ornate plasterwork of the ballrooms inside. Stars who have played and stayed at the Midland range from Laurel and Hardy to the Beatles and the Rolling Stones. Famous stage actor Sir Henry Irving died there in 1905, and almost every Prime Minister up to Harold Wilson has visited.

Sculptures

THE Victorians knew the value of a good piece of public art. If a city was proud of its sons and daughters, then a statue was in order. Bradford has some wonderful examples of statuary of its most famous names, from J.B. Priestley to Richard Oastler to William Forster. In these modern times, however, representational sculpture has fallen somewhat out of fashion, unless for comedians or cricket players and paid for by public fund-raising. This has led to a proliferation of more intriguing pieces; artwork that, while not in the traditional mould, does cast an interesting light on life in Bradford today and the city's long and rich heritage. Thus, the wool industry is honoured with twisted steel fibres and gigantic needles, while those who lost their lives in the devastating Bradford city fire are also honoured. A sculpture trail has been set up to take in all these wonderful pieces of public art, and a leaflet can be obtained from tourist information centres or the internet.

Bradford's superb Cartwright Hall Museum (about which there is more detail later) has some excellent examples of sculpture in the surrounding Lister Park, including this marvellous bronze statue of the Roman Goddess of the Hunt, Diana, near the Princes Gate, along with this bold and powerful stag sculpture. Until the park underwent a restoration programme, the statue was covered in white paint.

The Bradford City fire disaster memorial in Centenary Square – a moving tribute to the 56 who died and more than 300 who were injured in the devastating events of May 1985.

Andy Hazell's 10ft light bulb sculpture, upended and planted in the ground at the entrance to the Forster Square retail park.

The World War One Memorial, near the Alhambra, which was unveiled on 1 July 1922 – the sixth anniversary of the first day of the Battle of the Somme, in which the Bradford 'Pals' regiment was all but wiped out.

Stationed outside the Law Courts off Drake Street, this curiously skeletal leaf is a homage to Bradford-born composer Frederick Delius. It was unveiled in 1993 and is meant to symbolise Delius's love of nature and his recurring themes of life, death and regeneration.

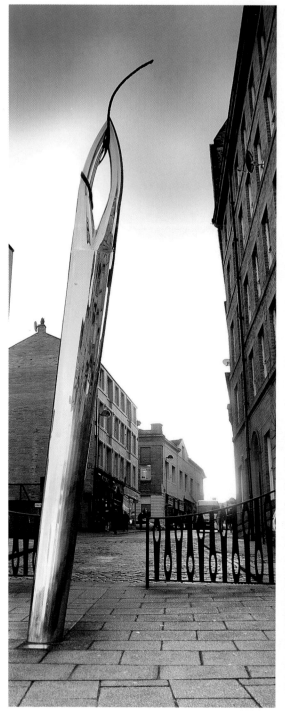

Opposite: Two views of the *Needle* on North Parade, which was unveiled in July 2000. Designed by Rick Faulkner, it has a double meaning; as well as paying homage to Bradford's heritage as the heart of the world textile industry, the needle – which is threaded – is also meant to symbolise the concept of an integrated transport system of rail and road connecting the city. The thread wrapped around the eye of the needle is made of fibre-optic material and is illuminated at night. The installation was quite controversial at the time of its unveiling.

Left: A more traditional example of sculpture but nonetheless controversial. It is, of course, Richard Oastler, the Bradford humanitarian who campaigned to save children from working exhaustingly – and often fatally – long hours for a pittance in wages. His campaign was vigorously opposed by the factory owners, who relied upon the cheap labour provided by the children. Oastler's concentration on the campaign led to a decline in his health, the loss of his job and a stint in debtors' prison. The statue was the result of public donations and is currently in its third home. It was first in Forster Square, then Rawson Square, and moved in 1968 near to John Street Market. Oastler died in 1861, and his statue was unveiled eight years later.

Left: The Questor was unveiled in June 1998 and is the work of sculptor Keith McCarter. It sits outside the Aldermanbury development, the home of the Thomas Cook travel agency offices, and is meant to symbolise Bradford's 'adventurous nature'.

Below: The statue of one John Boynton ('J.B.') Priestley, playwright of this parish, which was erected in 1986, two years after his death.

In 1904, three years after Victoria died, this epic sculpture was unveiled in Bradford by the then Prince of Wales, later to become King George V. It was the work of Alfred Drury, considered to be one of the most important sculptors of the time, who chose to depict Victoria in her prime as the ruler of the British Empire, in full state regalia with the crown on her head and sceptre and orb in her hands. Three tons of bronze were used to cast the 12ft-high statue, and 30,000 people turned out to watch the official unveiling on 4 May at the site off Little Horton Lane. The pedestal on which Victoria stands was the work of architect John William Simpson, who also worked on Cartwright Hall and, further afield, the old Wembley Stadium.

If you cut down off Manor Row towards Forster Square train station and retail park you will be met by these intriguingly engineered pieces of sculpture in St Blaise Square. They are formed from railway tracks, twisting out of the ground and set in stone paving. Perspex tubing inside the sculptures illuminates them at night. The sculpture, by Ian Randall, is also evocative of Bradford's wool-combing past; indeed, St Blaise Square is named after the Patron Saint of this industrial practice.

PUBLIC houses play an important part in the history of any community. They were where the workers relaxed after long days in the mills, where social reform was hammered out, where love affairs blossomed...and, to be fair, where marriages ended. Bradford University professor Paul Jennings recently published a book on the social history of the British pub, entitled *The Local*. Combining in his study the pub's importance in any town or city with the latter-day concerns about drink-fuelled violence and crime, he said 'My research has taken me to some depressing places and I've witnessed some dispiriting behaviour, but the pub has also provided me with real pleasure.' Of course, Bradford's drinkers also had to cope with the Temperance movement of the 19th century, and looming large among those calling time on the drinking classes was social reformer and mill owner Titus Salt. Whether he would be amused to find 21st-century Bradford has a pub named after him is difficult to say.

Examples of some of Bradford's popular and long-standing pubs, including the Boy & Barrel on Westgate, which is also the location of The Star, and the Mill Lane pub, formerly a Royal Airforce Association club.

The City Vaults pub on Hustlergate in the city centre. As its name suggests, it was a former bank building, and its history is cheekily referenced by a couple of mannequins dressed up like bank robbers, who currently adorn the interior of the pub.

The New Beehive on Westgate, a favourite of real ale drinkers and jazz aficionados. It was built in 1901 and is thought to be the last gas-lit pub in the country.

Lister's free house on Manchester Road, named, of course, after Bradford woolman Samuel Lister.

Nestled just off the roundabout at the top of Hall Ings is the Jacob's Well pub, a real throwback to the days of the good, old-fashioned community boozer, although the community it historically served has been replaced by city-centre development.

The Cock and Bottle on Barkerend Road – once designated a 'Christian' pub in 1999, where the Bishop of Bradford would take services!

Wool Exchange

OCCUPYING the space at the bottom of Darley Street, the Wool Exchange is one of Bradford's hidden gems. Now housing the local branch of the book-selling chain Waterstone's, which makes a point of trying to find interesting homes for its outlets, one can spend as much time looking up at the incredible vaulted ceiling as you can browsing through the books. It was constructed in the 1860s, with Lord Palmerston, the then Prime Minister, laying the foundation stone. As the name suggests, it was originally a trading area for the wool industries of the time and would have buzzed with traders and sponsored members wandering around the floor, striking verbal deals that were later ratified on paper.

A wonderful view of the Flemish-influenced tower and one of the building's doorways, constructed in the Venetian Gothic style.

Look up from your coffee in the Starbucks franchise on the mezzanine floor and prepare to have your breath taken away.

One of the many pieces of sculpture inside the building.

An example of the church-style glass windows used in the Wool Exchange.

The ornate staircase from the ground floor to the mezzanine.

Outside, by the entrance, is this statue of King Edward III – a great supporter of the wool trade.

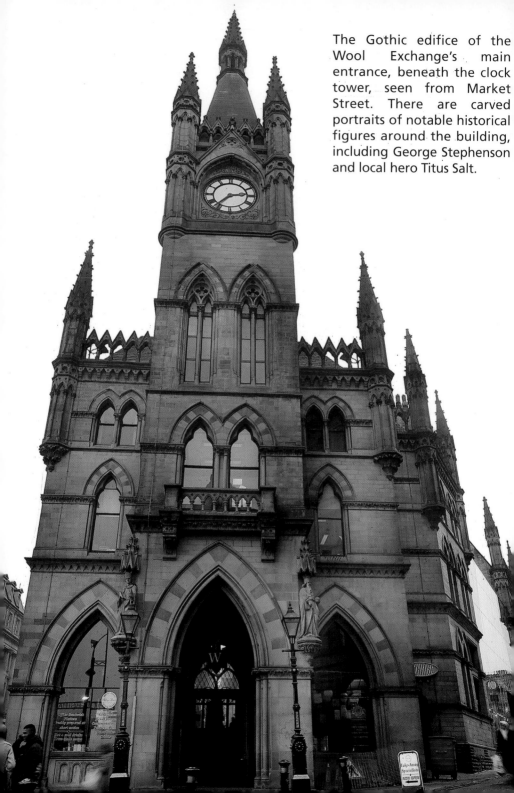

The Gothic edifice of the Wool Exchange's main entrance, beneath the clock tower, seen from Market Street. There are carved portraits of notable historical figures around the building, including George Stephenson and local hero Titus Salt.

Pictured here are the explorer Captain James Cook *(top)* and the fêted navigator Christopher Columbus *(below).*

Sir Francis Drake *(top)* and Sir Walter Raleigh *(below)*.

Theatres

THE theatrical tradition in Bradford is very strong, with two main council-controlled venues, St George's Hall and the Alhambra, plus the smaller independent theatres such as The Priestley and the Theatre in the Mill. There is also a grand tradition of community-based theatre from companies such as Mind the Gap, Kala Sangam and Lost Dog. Of course, in the past there were many more venues, including the Theatre Royal, where famed thespian Sir Henry Irving was coming to the end of a run in *Becket* in 1905 when he took ill and died at the Midland Hotel. The Priestley is housed in a former Temperance Hall, which became the Bradford Civic Playhouse in 1927. It suffered serious fires in 1935 and 1996. The Empire Theatre on Great Horton Road closed down in 1916, two years after the rival Alhambra opened across the road. The Prince's Theatre was demolished in the 1970s, and the Palace lasted from 1875 to 1938. But the tradition is alive and well, attracting some of the best of the touring shows to the main venues. And as long as that happens, the show will go on...

Originally built as a music hall in 1914, the year World War One started, the Alhambra has endured as one of Bradford's great landmarks, attracting theatre audiences from across the North and beyond. It has a capacity of 1,650 and was partially rebuilt in the mid-1980s. It is the home of Bradford's traditional festive pantomime, and it was modelled on the Moorish designs of its Spanish namesake in Granada. The Alhambra is at its most beautiful and powerful by night, with the lavish lighting projecting the excitement of the theatre like a beacon.

Shown here is the scale of the huge theatre.

The dizzyingly cavernous central dome from the inside.

It was Queen Victoria who officially opened St George's Hall on 29 August 1853. The building of the theatre had been proposed more than four years before, and a good portion of the £35,000 cost of the building was raised through £10 shares sold to the public. Those who have since passed through its portals make up nothing less than a fascinating account of British history in the past century and a half. Within a year of St George's opening, Charles Dickens gave his first ever public reading of *Bleak House* there. The famous escapologist Harry Houdini carried out his amazing feats in 1905, and five years later Winston Churchill held a political meeting there...and faced a stage invasion from suffragettes.

An example of the carved stonework on the outside of the building.

The door to the stage bar.

More examples of the intricate carvings on the exterior of St George's Hall.

St George's Hall was taken into the ownership of Bradford Council in 1949 and a modernisation programme began. It was officially opened in 1953, with a new £8,000 organ and a flexible stage. In 1982 a fire broke out and caused severe damage to the roof, prompting a further £2 million refurbishment programme. The venue was closed for three months in 2003 when cracks were discovered in the ceiling. Now it can accommodate almost 1,900 people, seated and standing.

Little Germany is the home of The Priestley, an independent theatre that welcomes touring productions and artists, as well as staging original shows by Bradford companies. In recent years, tragedy seems to have had an edge over comedy as The Priestley has had several financial hiccups, but still it fights on and remains a powerful force for independent theatre.

Below and overleaf: The famous mural celebrating the formation of the Independent Labour Party, which is on the wall of the Priestley.

The frontage of the theatre.

SOME of the most varied museums in the county are established in the Bradford district. From the traditional and awe-inspiring Cartwright Hall in Lister Park to the new city-centre Bradford 1 Gallery in Centenary Square, the past is brought well and truly alive in Bradford. As you might expect, there is a strong tradition of preserving Bradford's heritage of wool and engineering, especially at the innovative Industrial Museum, which has permanent displays of spinning and engineering equipment and early motor vehicles. Then there is historic Bolling Hall, where the Earl of Newcastle was told to 'pity poor Bradford' by a ghostly visitation when he was about to lay siege to the Parliament-supporting city, and the Colour Museum, which utilises the dyeing and colouring techniques of the textile industry to great effect. And, of course, there is the National Media Museum, formerly the National Museum of Photography, Film and Television, which attracts audiences from across the country with exhibitions, displays and the annual film festival.

Justifiably seen as the jewel in the crown of Bradford's civic museums, Cartwright Hall is a wonderful example of an architectural movement started right here in the city: Bradford Baroque. Standing in Lister Park, it was designed by the same architects who created Glasgow's famous Kelvingrove Art Gallery and was named after Edmund Cartwright, the inventor of the wool-combing machine that proved so crucial in building Bradford's industrial reputation. It was opened in 1904, and its first collections were made up of Victorian and Edwardian art donated by Samuel Lister.

Details of the stonework and columns that adorn the grand structure of the Cartwright Hall.

One could almost spend as long gazing at the intricate architecture that decorates the building as looking at the works of art within, which include old masters, modern painters and collections of Islamic art. And for all those who think art galleries are stuffy and boring, a piece of trivia: the Monty Python team filmed a musical number here for their 1983 movie *The Meaning of Life*.

The tower and statues that stand sentry on it. Most of the stone for Cartwright Hall was quarried in Idle.

From North Park Road, these vast and impressive gates give access to Lister Park and Cartwright Hall. The elaborate wrought ironwork was commissioned to commemorate the Bradford Exhibition of 1904, an event built around the completion of Cartwright Hall. Experts from Kew Gardens helped to set up a botanical display. There were recreations of naval battles with working models, and perhaps most notable was the creation of an African village, with 100 Somalis giving demonstrations of wrestling and spear-throwing. Close to the gates there is an Italianate lodge, which is a Grade II listed building.

Diana, the Roman name for Artemis, the Greek Goddess of the Hunt, takes centre stage in this panoramic shot of Cartwright Hall. The hall was officially opened in 1904 by the Prince and Princess of Wales, who also did the ribbon-cutting honours on an industrial exhibition within Lister Park. Before Cartwright Hall was built, the home of the Lister family stood just to the east of it. The old building was demolished in 1903 to make way for the new development. A lake, fed by a stream, winding through the botanical gardens, was one of the first features to be implemented in the Lister Park, which surrounded Cartwright Hall. It is in the serpentine style, with four islands.

Previous page and above: The National Media Museum. With almost 700,000 visitors a year and contributing tens of millions of pounds to the Bradford economy, it is one of the greatest assets the city has.

Lister's Mill

LOCATED in the heart of Manningham, Lister's Mill has been central to Bradford's development for a century and a half. From its origins as one of the powerhouses of the city's textile industry to its current use as top-specification apartments, this behemoth of a building has been an integral part of the Bradford landscape for generations. The brainchild of entrepreneur Samuel Lister, it was built to replace a former building called Manningham Mills, which was destroyed by fire in 1871. At the height of its production, an amazing 11,000 people worked there, producing top-end fabrics such as velvet and silk. When it opened in 1873, it was the largest textile mill in the North. Among the customers who purchased its wares were King George V, who took 1,000 yards of velvet for his coronation, and later the US President Gerald Ford, who wanted new velvet curtains for his stint in the White House. During World War Two, any flyer who bailed out of his Spitfire or Hurricane in the Battle of Britain would probably have floated to safety, owing to a silk parachute made at Lister's. These days, thanks to the innovative Manchester-based design company Urban Splash, Lister's Mill is alive once more, this time as apartments in part of Bradford's ongoing regeneration.

Pretty much wherever you stand in Bradford, you can see the chimney on Lister's Mill. At 255ft high, it is an imposing landmark and testimony to Samuel Lister's vaulting ambition and entrepreneurship...not for a lack of boldness is his name honoured in Bradford, nor for want of bravery was he known as the King of Velvet and a multi-millionaire.

More examples of the building's Italianate style and, over the entrance, Lister's motto: *Fidem parit integritas* – Integrity produces confidence.

Samuel Lister lives on at Lister's Mill...in statuary form, at least. The statue (*above left*) shows Lister sitting on a bale of the product that made him rich. There is a more famous statue of him in Lister Park, the space he donated to the city, in which he is depicted with a two-foot rule clutched across his chest.

Left: The pigeons that take their rest on the rooftops and carvings do not care whether the building is used for commerce or living, although it is much quieter these days.

Pages 163–168: The true scale of this industrial leviathan of a mill can be seen in all its glory, both close up and from a distance.

Saltaire

SALTAIRE...the creation of Titus Salt, considered to be one of the most enlightened and humanitarian industrialists of the 19th century. The town he gave his name to is considered to be one of the finest examples of the model village in the country. Salt decided to move his entire mill operation from Bradford to this land near Shipley, so he could have better transport links via the canals and the railways. He also wanted his workplace to be more accessible to his workers. To that end, he built new stone houses for them, baths and wash houses with running water, a hospital, a gymnasium, a park and a boathouse on the banks of the River Aire. Today, such is its importance that Saltaire has been classed as a World Heritage Site, along with the Pyramids in Egypt. Salt's vast mill is now home to a combination of bohemian and hi-tech businesses, and the narrow streets of terraced houses are in high demand.

Overleaf: A stunning aerial shot of Saltaire, a bird's-eye view of Titus Salt's great dream come true, which the progressive mill owner would doubtless have been thrilled to be able to see.

The traditional cobbled streets of Saltaire, still preserved.

The classic Victorian architecture of Victoria Hall.

Salt's Mill is the focus for coach-loads of tourists every day, especially because of its collection of David Hockney works. The Bradford-born painter was much enamoured of Saltaire.

Even the stone lions outside Victoria Hall seem in good humour and satisfied with their lot.

Two views of the United Reformed Church off Victoria Road. Formerly known as the Congregational Church, it has the highest level of protection available to listed buildings. Sir Titus, who died in 1876, is interred in the mausoleum adjacent to the church.

Salt's Mill seen in its impressive entirety.

Victoria Hall, built in 1871 as the home for the Saltaire Club and Institute. Today, it is used for theatrical productions and shows.

The canal at Saltaire is a wonderful place to spend a relaxing afternoon…especially as just beyond that bridge, at the bottom of Victoria Road, is the Boathouse pub.

The Saltaire Train Station, near to the mill.

As parking spaces might be at a premium on Saltaire's narrow streets, it is sometimes better to get about by bike, as this chap is proving.

A typical Saltaire front door.

With the demand for homes in Saltaire being high, and no prospect of cramming new houses in thanks to its heritage status, developers have had to think laterally...or vertically. Existing buildings are now being used to create new apartments, as is the case with this scheme.

A denizen of Saltaire takes it easy.

THIS has been a book of buildings and architecture, but behind every stone laid, every piece of marble sculpted, and every home lived in, there lies a human life. For a city that grew at the rate Bradford did, there needed to be a place for those who had earned their eternal rest to reside. And that place was Undercliffe Cemetery. The Bradford Undercliffe Cemetery Company was formed following the purchase of a large manor house and grounds in 1851. William Gay was employed to design and landscape this vast necropolis, and the first burials took place in 1854 under the stewardship of Gay, who stayed on as registrar and manager of this 25-acre cemetery. The rich, of course, were delighted and saw the establishment of Undercliffe as a way to ensure some measure of immortality, through extravagant mausoleums and tombs. For the best part of a century, the cemetery operated as private concern, but in 1977 the Bradford Undercliffe Cemetery Company went into liquidation. Bradford Council was unwilling to take it on as a municipal cemetery, and two years later it was sold to a developer for the sum of just £5. The once grand cemetery fell prey to vandals until, in 1984, the Council realised the importance of the site, compulsorily purchased it, and its renovation began. Now, Undercliffe Cemetery is listed by the English Heritage Register of Parks and Gardens of Special Historic Interest, and it is maintained by volunteers and the Undercliffe Cemetery Charity.

It seems a foreboding place at times, but that has not stopped many, many people using Undercliffe Cemetery as a facility for research, photographic projects or even just walking around, reading the gravestones and ruminating on Bradford's past.

Undercliffe's atmospheric avenues and obelisks have also attracted film makers. The classic 1960s adaptation of Keith Waterhouse's *Billy Liar* was partially shot in the cemetery, and in 1997 David Tennant – who later shot to fame as Doctor Who – appeared in the movie *LA Without A Map*, about the love between a funeral director and an American girl he meets in a cemetery. The following pages show the true beauty of Undercliffe Cemetery and the record of history that is etched on every headstone. Take the opportunity for a few quiet moments of contemplation as you view the plots and tombs of this marvellous place.

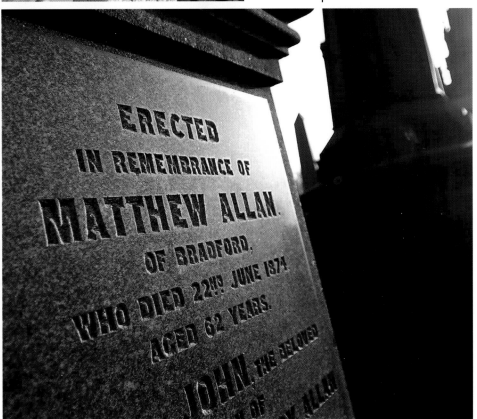

A sobering chapter to close upon, you might think, but not necessarily. As the sun sets upon the Gothic magnificence of Undercliffe Cemetery, it is true that this picture might remind us of our own mortality and our own brief time upon the earth. However, we should also remember that the thousands who are laid to rest in Undercliffe have all, in ways big or small, helped to shape the Bradford we see around us today. Perhaps they were industrialists or business magnates who put Bradford on the map, or maybe they were ordinary people who worked in the mills and offices, kept homes, swept the streets, drew their wages and spent them in Bradford's shops and pubs. At the beginning of this book it was suggested that a city that stands still is a city that dies. Every life lived in Bradford helps Bradford to survive, and long after all of us are gone we can be sure that Bradford will ultimately endure.

Subscribers

Steve Abbott
Mr Harry Ackroyd
Paul Richard Ackroyd
Geoffrey Allan
Annabelle Appleyard
Francesca Appleyard
Samantha Appleyard

Harry Baker
Carlo Baranyai
Gillian Baranyai
Bill Barraclough
Philip James Barraclough
Gordon Barrett
Mrs Edith Bates
Geoff Baxter
Martin Baxter
John Beaumont
Alan K. Biggin
Christopher & Kay Binns
Trudi Blackburn
Josef Peter Bodnarczuk
John Ellis Booker
Catherine Boltwood
Graham Anthony Booth
Mark Adrian Booth
Nigel Paul Booth
Thomas John Booth
David Bould
John Boyle
Derek Brayshaw
Gladys Brayshaw
Maria Brearton
Lynne Briggs
Susan Brigg
R. & M. Brookman (Nailsea, Somerset)
Marie Brosch
Stan & Sheila Burnham
Sidney William Burrows
Nigel & Diane Burton
Hartley Butler
Chris Butterfield
Jean Butterfield
Roger Butterfield

Michael D. Carter
Richard S. Carter
Stephen & Jennifer Cashman
Joanne Chadwick
Alice Chapman
William J. Chapman
Linda Chiappetta
Donald Clapham
Ann & Colin Clark

Joan & Willie Clark
Pauline A. Clark
Olwen Clarke
Amos Clarkson
Mr & Mrs Alan & Sandra Clayton
Mrs Joyce Clifford
S. G. Collier
Catharine Hilda Cook
George Wilfred Cook
John Cook
Pat Cooper
Rita Crabbe
Dorothy Cranmer
John Cranmer
Angela S. Crompton
Clifford Hartley Crompton
Ethel W. Crompton
Brian S. Crossland

B. Danylczuk
Derek Dawson
Olive Mary Dawson
Eric Dean
Gordon Dean
Robert Denney
Betsy Dennis
B. Denton
B. K. Denton
May Dickinson
Ron & Jean Dodd
Ian Dolby
Peter Dolby
Winifred Dolby
Marie Dorman
Mr Peter Drabble
Mrs Florence Dunn

Peter Eastaugh
Elite Top Guards Ltd
Harry Ellis
Ronald Ellis (Australia)
E.T.G. Training Services Ltd
Leslie Evans
Leslie Anthony Evans
Jeffrey James Eyre

Mrs Shirley Farrell
Ivy Farrington
David Fenton
Bernard & Anne Flanagan
George Ford
Cecil Fowler
Ian G. Fox
Gordon Foxall

Kenneth Frost
Mr Roy Furby

John Galert
Victor Galert
Joyce Gaunt
Peter Gaunt
Brian & Jennifer Gilbert
Laraine Gill
Neil Gill
Stephen Gill
H. Glover
Aubrey Brian Goodyear
Bernard Grant
Norman Grant
Raymond Grant
John T. Gray
Mrs Dorothy Greenwood
Olive Grice
Barry Gudgeon

Emily Hale
Peter Haley
Graham Hall
Margaret Hall
Philip Hall
Mrs Denise Hall
Edward Trevor Hall
Dorothy Hardwick
Christopher Harrison
John Harrison
Roseleen Harrison
Mrs Norma Hartley
Wilfred Harvey (1921-1997)
Peter Haynes
Robert Haynes
Samantha Haynes
Susan Haynes
Peter Hayton
Amy Heenan
John Heenan
Arthur Hemingway
Brian Hemingway
Geoffrey Holden
Derek & Patricia Holmes
James Allan Holroyd
Leslie Hooson
Andrew David Horrocks
Elizabeth Horan
John Francis Horan
Doreen Hosty
Jack Howie
Joan Howie
Josh Howie
Ada Hudson (1920-2008)

Hadrian H. Hudson
Kevin Hudson
Sydney Hudson (1917-1981)
Ivor & Maureen Hughes
Malcolm & Janet Hughes
Shirley Hughes

David Martin Illingworth
Eric & Irene Illingworth
Margot Illingworth

Nicola Jarvis
M. Jenkinson (Australia)
Roy Jenkinson
Arthur Johnston
Bob Johnson
Edward & Mavis Johnson
Mollie Johnson
Walter Johnson
Dorothy Jowett (Canada)
Ruth & Bob Jowett (Canada)

Kevin Keenan
Terry Keeys
Stella Keyte
David King
John Robinson Kirby
Jack & Dorothy Knowles
Margaret Krupa

Anne & Rodney Lacey
Mrs Margaret Lancaster
Mr Peter Lancaster
Dr Philip Roy Lancaster
Barry Campbell Lane
Marc Lawrence
Donald & Mary Lightowler
Norman Littlewood
Roy Lowther
Katalin E. Lukacs

Carol Macfarlane (née Mann)
Harrison Maximiliano
Mackin
Alan Mainwaring
Karl David Mandreit
Anthony Mann
Edna Marshall
Stanley & Pauline Mawson
Michael McCabe
Ron & Shirley McCabe & Jaz
Patrick McCreesh
Freda McNiff
Andrew Metcalfe
Mrs Gertrude Metcalfe
Cpl Ian Metcalfe
Albert Mills RIP
Christine Mills
Eileen Mills (née Bergin) RIP
Phillis Mills RIP

Tommy Mirfield
(Barnoldswick)
D. Mitchell
Nancy Mitchell
Joan S. Moorhouse
W. David Moorhouse
George Morgan
Iain Morris
Shirley Morris
Terence Gordon Morris
Beatrice Muldowney
Lynne Murrell

Francis Graham Naylor
Shirley Mary Naylor
J. Lewis Nicholl I.Eng.,
M.I.E.T.

Laird Graham O' Keefe Binns
Boyd O'Brien
Brenda O'Brien
Lucky O'Brien
Julie Catharine Oliver

Donald Greenwood Pickles
Sheila Pittock
Mr Stephen G Potter
Marion Potterton
Norman Priestley

Jeanette Ramsden
Vivienne Rendall
David Rhodes
Linda Richardson
Mr A. Robertshaw
Bob & Jess Rushforth
Bryan Russell
Elsy Russell (née Joyce)
Kim Russell-Cooper
Brendan Russell-Cooper
Joseph Ryan
Mary Ryan

Fred Scott
Jack Scott
Raymond Scott
Rosamond Scott
Michael Senior
Peter & Barbara Shaw
Samuel Shaw
Alan Simpson
Gwenn Simpson
Terry Slingsby
Joyce Smith (Great Horton)
Susan Smith (née Wright)
Tracy Smith
Hubert Spencer
Joe Spencer
Percy Spencer

Paul Stephenson
Thomas Stork
Joan Sturdy
Jane Summerscales
John Summerscales
Reneé Summerscales
Mr Ian P. & Mrs Jill Sutcliffe
Keith & Mrs Audrey E.
Sutcliffe
Simon A. & Mrs Dawn P.
Sutcliffe
Harry Sweeney

Enid Taylor
Paul Tesseyman
Adam Tewkesbury
David Tewkesbury
Brenda Thomas
Alan David Thompson
Jean Thompson (née Stobbs)
Andrew McLean Thomson
Kirstie Tinsley
Geoffrey Toothill
Touchstone Centre
James Turner

Mary Walker
Tom Walker
Sheila Warren
Arthur Watson
Bob Watson
Patricia Watson
Kenneth A. Webster
A. Paul Whitaker
Mary Whitcombe
Krystina White
Sheila & Jack Widdop
Bernard Wilkinson
Brian Arthur Wilkinson
Henry Wilkinson
Muriel Elaine Wilkinson
Roger Ian Wilkinson
Keith Wilks
Pauline Ann Wilks
Eric Wilson
Maureen Wilson
Olive Wilson
Peter Windle
Mrs Mary Wood
Les Woodcock
In Memory of May Woodcock
Peter Worger
Mrs Audrey Worley
Paul David Stephen Wright
The late Robert Wright MBE
Liam Peter Laurence Wyatt
Paul Wyatt
Peter Joseph Wyatt

Malcolm Yearsley

Would you like one of the pictures in this book hanging on your wall?

Or perhaps you'd like to give one as a gift?

Almost all the pictures in this book are available to buy in a variety of different sizes and on a wide array of gifts and mementos, including calendars, mugs, jigsaws, mouse-mats, drinks coasters, T–shirts, fridge magnets and key rings

All you need to do to order is log on to our website:

www.telegraphandargus.co.uk

and click on the "View and Buy Photos" button.

Or you can visit our Reception Counter at the Telegraph & Argus, Hall Ings, Bradford. Telephone 01274 705275

Other pictures taken by our award-winning photographers are uploaded daily onto our website for you to browse and buy online. They include news events, sports action and a host of other interesting and exciting images. You will also find aerial views of the district, pictures from the past and a wide selection of scenic photographs.